I KNOW WHAT IT LOOKS LIKE

but I Choose to Believe God

EVELYN CARTWRIGHT

Copyright © 2020 by Evelyn Cartwright

All rights reserved.

No part of this book may be reproduced in any form or by any electronic or mechanical means, including information storage and retrieval systems, without written permission from the author, except for the use of brief quotations in a book review.

Cover photo courtesy of The Christian Broadcasting Network

ISBN 978-1-950123-42-1

Teresa Skinner Publishers

Contents

Introduction	v
The Diagnosis	1
The Process	10
God Working in Mysterious Ways	18
I Know What it Looks Like	21

Introduction

"Mrs. Cartwright, I've got some good news, and I've got some bad news. The bad news is there is a tumor on your brain. The good news is the tumor is not cancerous." That is what the doctor said to me. Those words took me on a journey that changed my life forever. By the end of the journey, my faith had become unshakable, and my relationship with the Lord was closer than it had ever been. It was through faith in God that I experienced his miraculous healing power.

The intent of this testimony is to bring inspiration or to spark hope and ignite faith in the lives of individuals facing what appears to be, or what they believe to be, an impossible situation. It is my belief that through the word of God faith can be increased to a level that produces blessings and miracles. If you are faced with a challenge that seems impossible, I can tell you from personal experience that with God all things are possible. There is absolutely nothing too hard for him. Mark 9:23 says, "Jesus said unto him, if thou canst believe, all things are possible to him that believeth." By his supernatural power, faith in God makes the impossible possible.

At some point a decision to totally trust God with your life has to be made. Will you choose to believe what God's word has to say about what you are facing or will you choose to believe other sources? Going through my challenge believing God and what his word said rather than what circumstances projected was my choice.

Faith in God is what the enemy of our soul does not want us to have. It is the means by which victory is attained. That is why he distorts vision and magnifies challenges to make them appear bigger than our God. Please believe that our God is greater than anything Satan brings our way. For me, developing unwavering faith was a process, but today I am healed, delivered, and set free by faith in the unmatchable power of God!

God is no respecter of persons. What he has done for others, he will do for you. I pray this testimony inspires you to give God a chance at what you, doctors, and others have deemed impossible. There is a song that says, "When you've tried everything and everything has failed, try Jesus." Jesus should not be our last choice, my recommendation is that you give him a try.

The Diagnosis

While relaxing one Sunday evening, the most excruciating pain hit me in the top of my head and traveled behind my right eye. It was so unbearable that it led to a trip to the emergency room. My best description is that it felt like someone hitting the top of my head repeatedly with a hammer or some extremely heavy object and stabbing me in my right eye with a sharp knife. When I clutched my head between my hands, the throbbing and pulsating pounded like the rhythm of an erratic heartbeat. On a scale of one to ten, the level of pain was off the chart. There was not a doubt in my mind that immediate medical attention was necessary.

On the ride to the ER, the pain continued to intensify, so much so that I started wondering if I would live to get there. Although fear gripped my heart, upon arriving at the ER, there was a small sense of relief knowing I made it to a place where I could possibly be helped.

The nurse sitting at the front desk grabbed a wheelchair for me and immediately started the intake process. After gathering some information, she pushed me around a corner, behind a curtain, to check my vitals. She discovered my blood pressure was 213/123. That was concerning. By then, my right eye was running like a faucet, and in so much pain, it would not stay open. In less than five minutes, someone took me to an exam room.

The doctor showed up. He asked me several questions and did a physical assessment. Once that was completed, he gave the nurse orders to start an IV to administer morphine and other medications to relieve the pain and lower my blood pressure; he also ordered a head/brain CT.

In about an hour, the result was in. The doctor walked over to my bedside and said, "Mrs. Cartwright, the scan shows a mass on your brain, but we aren't able to determine what the mass is. What I would like to do is admit you and get an MRI to get a better look and figure out what this mass is."

It was unbelievable and quite frustrating that I was in the hospital, had a brain scan, and still didn't know what was wrong with me. I was expecting to have some answers after the test result was in, but it only raised more questions. Wondering what in the world could be so bad that the doctors couldn't figure it out brought on more anxiety and caused fear to escalate.

The MRI was ordered for the next morning. Meanwhile, it got very late. My family and the doctor left, and I was alone with my thoughts and imagination running wild, trying to come up with a possible self-diagnosis. In retrospect, I wondered what in the world made me think I could do what the professionals had not been able to do.

Eventually, the meds knocked me out, and the next thing I knew it was morning. I fell asleep thinking about the MRI and finding out what was wrong with me. Not long after opening my eyes, my heart began pounding in my chest, and my stomach felt like it was twisted in knots. The order for the MRI was in, and the anxiety of waiting to be picked up for the MRI kicked in. After what seemed like forever but was actually two hours, someone came to get me. Once the MRI was completed, there was more waiting. Every kind of scenario and diagnosis ran through my mind. None of which was good.

Around two hours later, a different doctor than the one from the night before walked into the room with papers in his hands. He introduced himself and said he had the test results. He then walked across the room, sat down in a chair, and crossed his legs. As I watched him thumbing through the papers, everything around me slowed down to the speed of a movie playing in slow motion. Nothing in my entire life had ever made me so anxious.

The doctor opened his mouth and began to speak; he couldn't get to it fast enough for me. The words he said will forever be etched in my memory. He looked directly into my eyes and said, "Mrs. Cartwright, I've got some good news, and I've got some bad news. The bad news is that there is a tumor on your brain. The good news is the tumor is not cancerous."

I heard every word he said but could not, for the life of me, wrap my mind around the fact that he was talking to me about me. So many thoughts bombarded my mind that I wanted to shut it off, but it was like trying to shut off a dripping water faucet. No matter how hard the handle is turned, it keeps dripping.

At that moment the terms stunned or devastated could not begin to describe my feelings; as a matter of fact, I deemed both words gross understatements and completely inadequate to describe my feelings. My head desperately struggled to process what my ears had just heard. Never in a million years would I have expected that kind of news! This was one of those things that always happened to someone else, but this time it was me. I was the someone else. The news left me feeling dazed.

I laid back on the bed, shaking my head in disbelief. The doctor asked if I was alright. The word yes automatically came out of my mouth, but that wasn't true. He sat there for a few more minutes and told me he was discharging me with a referral to see a neurologist, and the neurologist would come up with a plan for treatment. He wished me well and then left the room. My emotions vacillated between distress and gratefulness. Distress because of just being diagnosed with a tumor on my brain, yet grateful because the tumor was not cancerous. For years, I had suffered with debilitating headaches and had always attributed it to migraines and hypertension. The thought never crossed my mind that it could be something as serious as a tumor on my brain.

When the daunting task of sharing the diagnosis with my children came to mind, that brought on more anxiety. It was a much-dreaded job but had to be done. This news would shake them beyond belief. My children and I are inseparable, especially after the death of my son, their older brother. Our closeness supersedes many parent and child relationships. For all of their lives, we've only had each other. We often tell each other that all we have is each other. To face the possibility that one of us not might be around anymore, I was afraid would be more than any of us could bear.

My heart ached for them even more than for myself. I decided to tell them exactly how the doctor told me with the good news, bad news statement. When I told them, they put up a brave front for my benefit. While I appreciated the effort, I saw through them as clearly as looking through a plate of glass. Things they never verbalized could be seen in their eyes. Reading them as only a mother can read her child, fear and pain was obvious in their faces.

We had often joined forces to face many challenge, but never anything of this magnitude. The only thing worse was the death of my eldest son. My children along with a few friends supported and continually prayed for me. Everyone constantly reassured me that everything would be alright. The depth of my children's concern was apparent. My daughter was working a full-time job, driving an hour to work each way and then thirty more minutes to get to my house, but managed to show up almost every day to spend hours with me and do whatever needed to be done.

My son lived in California and was in Arizona on a regular basis. He traveled back and forth so much I couldn't believe it. My daughter contacted him the night I was hospitalized. Early the next morning, he walked into my room. Watching them, I knew I could not allow myself to crumble because if I did all of us would. It's amazing how love gives you strength, courage, and fuel to fight even when you don't feel like it. I fought for all of us.

To add to the trauma, my husband could not provide the support I so desperately needed from him. He was suffering with dementia and had been diagnosed as terminally ill with other diseases that had affected every major organ in his body. There were days when he seemed to understand, and then there were times that he did not recognize me at all. So, through no fault of his own, he could not be there for me. Taking all things into consideration, it would have been an unrealistic expectation on my part. My heart yearned for it, but my mind accepted the fact that I would never have his support. It was a very mentally and emotionally trying time.

Even after being diagnosed and during treatment, the job of being his caretaker did not stop for me. When he took his last breath, I was with him. To be honest, sometimes between what he was going through, some days I functioned well, and on others not so well.

Had it not been for the strength, mercy, and grace of God, I would not have survived it all. I realized it was not my strength that I walked in. 2 Corinthians 12:9 a says, "And he said unto me, my grace is sufficient for thee; my strength is made perfect in weakness." It would have been impossible to survive this experience had it not been for the Lord, who was on my side. He empowered me to continue when it didn't seem possible to do so. God has been and continues to be extremely good to me.

He was always there for me. When my body was physically exhausted, God strengthened me. He kept my mind. He is the only reason I maintained my sanity. That's why my heart is filled with gratitude for what the Lord did for me. God brought me through it all victoriously!

To continue with the healing testimony, when my family and I saw the neurologist, we had no idea we were about to be hit with more unbelievable news. As if the news of a tumor on my brain wasn't bad enough, that day we were told that because of where the tumor was located, it was inoperable.

The neurologist and his associates determined that surgery would do more damage than good and possibly cause the loss of sight in my right eye. Since surgery was not an option, the recommendation was to try and shrink the tumor with radiation. I asked the neurologist how long he thought the tumor had been there, and he told me it was a very slow growing tumor. He suspected it had been there at least twenty years. Once again, my ears heard what he said, but my mind couldn't wrap itself around this new information. However, in the grand scheme of things, I was incredibly grateful to still be alive.

This news caused me to wonder if the tumor was a death

sentence for me. My thought was if the tumor didn't kill me, then all the medication might. In my opinion, I was functioning better before all the meds. How crazy is it when you are prescribed meds but are given more meds to help you with sickness from the original meds? Crazy!

After the diagnosis and after being told that the problem could not be solved with surgery, the enemy subtly crept in and shifted my focus from God my healer to the fact that there was an inoperable tumor on my brain. The problem appeared to have no solution. For a few weeks, the devil had me dwelling on that. Then suddenly one day out of the blue, God allowed me to recall something that had occurred two weeks prior to finding out about the tumor.

Two weeks earlier while in the presence of the Lord, I heard the words: "Your later shall be greater, and your best is yet to come!" Remembering those word redirected my mind to God and promises he had made me. Once I really began to think about that promise, the realization came that I had to live to receive it. I could not die and see the promise!

Rather than allow the devil to have control over my thoughts and let him kill me like he wanted to, I chose to refocus, get my mind back on God, and keep it there. I held on to what the Lord had reminded me of, took my eyes off of circumstances, and spoke life over myself, starting with Psalm 118:17 (KJV), "I shall not die, but live, and declare the works of the Lord." That was where the start of walking by faith, not by sight, really began for me on this journey.

In the beginning, the initial shock of hearing there was an inoperable tumor on my brain knocked me down. Thank God, it didn't knock me out, and God didn't allow me to stay down. He reminded me that I had promises to live for. With faith in Him and access to His grace and mercy, I was able to get back up again! In my mind was the image of a wrestling match. One wrestler had the other pinned to the mat, and the referee was counting. But before the referee hit the mat for what would be the last time, somehow that wrestler managed to shake the opponent off and reverse positions. He got on top, pinned the opponent down, and unexpectedly won the match.

I imagined myself pinned to the mat with the referee ready to hit the mat for the last count when somehow, I managed to shake my opponent off (Satan) and our positions are reversed. Rather than being on top, he ends up on the bottom, which was where he belonged in the first place. When we take our eye off God and focus on circumstances, we give the enemy the opportunity to get into a place that he was never meant be in. He was never meant to be on top. He was meant to be on the bottom under our feet!

I experienced what I call spiritual amnesia. My problem looked so big that for a minute I forgot to remember that I serve a big God, and there was nothing too hard for him. My problem looked so big that I forgot to remember that with God all things are possible. Thank God, the spiritual amnesia was only temporary.

After God delivered me from the temporary amnesia, my faith needed to be increased; it needed to be stronger than ever for what I was facing. God gave me some ways to fortify my faith and increase it. The Holy Spirit prompted me to search out scriptures on faith and healing, write them down, and read them aloud on a regular basis. That was the way to get them embedded in my spirit. The Bible says, "Faith comes by hearing and hearing by the word of God." Romans 10:17

Taking on the characteristics of a sponge, I began soaking up every word that was conducive to health and healing. My spirit was open to receive the word of God in many forms: attending church and conferences, listening to the word on the radio in the car, watching Christian television, reading books with positive messages, and reading the Bible.

For years, older saints would say, "Get the word, it's in the Word; everything you need is in the Word." I found that to be true. Eventually, my faith grew to the point that it didn't matter what the doctor said or what the situation looked like. I still believed in God! Once my faith was increased, I walked and lived in expectancy, expecting the doctor's report to change. Expecting God to heal me. Expecting to see the promises of God come to pass in my life.

With more faith, there was no room for doubters and negativity in my life. How I handled this situation would determine how those around me handled it. It was very important that the right atmosphere be set. An atmosphere of faith and total confidence in God. I refused to allow anything negative into my space because negativity, in this case, could bring death.

There was so much unfinished business inside of me that death was out of the picture. There was so much that I didn't want to take to a grave; there were books that had not been written, poems that hadn't been recited, sermons that had not been preached, and songs that had not been sung. There were assignments, appointments, and people to reach, touch, encourage, and inspire with a word and a testimony. There was still much work for me to do.

The Process

Although I had faith in God, my healing did not miraculously occur overnight. It was a process. You see, I really did not want to go through the radiation treatments and prayed that God would somehow miraculously heal me before the start date. That didn't happen, and it was disappointing. The Lord let me know me know that it had nothing to do with my faith. It was about His plan, His timing, and His way, not mine. What made me think I could dictate to God when and how to heal me? One day I realized that God already had a plan and a process to manifest my healing.

Just because I tried to impose time restrictions or a done by date didn't mean the promise was not coming in God's perfect time. Isaiah 55:8-9 says, "For my thoughts are not your thoughts, neither are your ways my ways, saith the Lord. For as the heavens are higher than the earth, so are my ways higher than your ways, and my thoughts than your thoughts." God's plan took me on a different route but arrived at the destination I wanted to reach.

The process started with radiation treatments. Although

prepped by the radiation oncologist and the staff, I could not imagine what it would be like. Days before the treatments were to begin the radiation oncologist made a mold of my face and the top of my head to create a mask. He told me it would be used to secure my head to the table during treatments. The first day of treatment, I was a bundle of nerves. The process had been explained, but my mind could not produce a clear picture of what it would really be like.

My first time in the treatment room, I saw this huge robotic looking machine that resembled a gigantic flying saucer in a science fiction movie. Up to this point, I had only read about it, seen pictures of it, and heard what the doctor had to say about it. To be in that room and see it in person was actually a lot to digest.

Picture this: I'm in a room lying on a table underneath this huge flying saucer looking machine. My face is masked, and my head is locked to the table while this machine is circling my head and beaming radiation to my brain. Not a pretty picture. Almost breath taking, but not in a good way. For five consecutive days, that was the process. That was day number one with four more to go.

The technician told me to bring something in to listen to the next day because it would help me relax and make the time go faster. My choice was some praise and worship music. I thought it would be played in my ears through a headset so no one else could hear it, but it was connected so the entire room was filled with the sound of praise and worship overhead!

That changed the atmosphere and shifted my focus. Now rather than lying there focusing on the radiation treatment, my focus shifted to praising and worshipping God. From that day to my last one there, every time I laid on that table, my heart and my mouth were filled with praise. I learned the true meaning of Psalm 34:1, which says, "I will bless the Lord at all times: his praise shall continually be in my mouth."

Many times that scripture is quoted, but this experience made me wonder if we really understand the depth of what we were saying when we quote it. Every word of that scripture came to life for me. That experience taught me how to truly bless the Lord at all times. Blessing him at a time like that assured me that it should not be a problem to bless him through anything, because victory was guaranteed!

MRI #1: After the last radiation treatment, the doctor gave me an appointment to see him in three months with instructions to get an MRI one week prior to the appointment. While I waited on the three months to pass, my prayer was that no tumor would show up on the MRI. My expectation was to hear good news, but at the appointment he told me the tumor was still there with no change and that he had not expected to see any change. Our expectations were totally different. Mine was for God to heal me. His was for no change. He said, "Let's wait another three more months and check again."

MRI#2: The time between visits seemed so long, but three months later, it was time to repeat the process. One week prior to the appointment, I went for the MRI and then went to see the doctor. During this visit, the doctor told me that the technician spotted something that he thought needed a closer look. He wanted to do another MRI that focused only on the right eye. Each time I had an MRI, I had to be given an IV for the contrast. I never looked forward to that.

MRI # 3: Same routine, get the MRI, then see the doctor. Only now the time increments were greatly decreased. Two doctor's visits and two MRIs in less than one month. When they slide me inside the machine this time, I closed my eyes and gave God praise and repeated Psalm 34:1 (KJV) over and over again. "I will bless the Lord at all times: his praise shall continually be in my mouth." Even with the sound of the machine, the praise inside my heart was much louder.

It only took two days to get the result. It appeared there was more going on than they had seen originally. They saw that the tumor was wrapped around my orbit, the socket the eye sits in. That made it appear worse at this point than from the beginning; however, I recognized that this was a trick of the devil. It was his attempt to get me to do what I had done in the very beginning, and that was to take my eyes off of Jesus and focus on the negative report. The devil wanted to shake my faith. I'm happy to report that his tactic did not work. It did not stop me from believing, and it did not stop my praise! The doctor told me that no additional radiation would be necessary because that area had already been targeted. No more radiation was good news in the midst of the bad news to me.

I continued to believe the report of the Lord. His report said in Isaiah 53:5, "But he was wounded for our transgressions, he was bruised for our iniquities: the chastisement of our peace was upon him; and with his stripes we are healed." When I told my daughter what the results showed, she said, "Don't worry about it, mama. That's just going to be a part of your testimony." She always had a very positive attitude. There were some people who did not.

Sometimes in order to stay positive and strong in faith, detaching from negative people will become necessary. Negative influence can contaminate your belief system. Faith and negativity cannot co-exist.

Shortly after that experience, one morning while lying in bed, the spirit of the Lord said, "It's time to stop praying and start praising. If you believe I have done what you asked me to do then stop praying about it and start praising." I heard those words as clear as day. From that moment, I didn't pray about the tumor ever again. Instead, I started praising. I had to tell all of the people who were praying for me to stop praying and start praising. People in several states were praying for me, and I had to contact them and give them the instructions God gave me. That way we would all be in agreement. "Can two walk together, except they be agreed?" Amos 3:3

When it was time to notify members of the church, I believed it would be best to do it corporately rather than individually. Upon my request and without questions or hesitation, the pastor gave me the opportunity to speak to the congregation on Sunday morning. The pastor's response assured me that God was opening the door to allow me to follow his instructions. Sometimes the instructions God gives might not make sense or might look or sound crazy to others, but God's instructions must be followed. I must admit that I did wonder what it was going to sound like telling people to stop praying for me. But when you trust God, you obey.

During a Sunday morning service, the pastor called me up and gave me the microphone. While standing before the congregation, I told them how much their prayers were appreciated, but I wanted them to stop praying for me. I informed them that if they'd like they could continue praying for me in other areas but do not pray about the tumor anymore. I explained that this was what the spirit of the Lord had instructed me to do. To stop praying and start praising and tell those that were praying for me to do the same; He said, "If I believed he had done what he said he would do then it was time to stop praying and start praising." As I imagined, there were some people who looked at me like I had lost my mind. They could not grasp why a person with a tumor on her brain would tell them not to pray for her anymore. Yes, it sounded a bit strange, but I had to obey God.

I Know What it Looks Like

Many times blessings and miracles are attached to our obedience. I wasn't taking any chances on missing my miracle. Some of the people looked at me like the tumor had affected my brain, and I had gone crazy... Obedience to God was more important than the opinions of people. This process taught me that following God's instructions is vitally important. It also taught me that not everyone is on the same level of faith. Some can receive and act on what others cannot.

The Pastor, his wife, and a few others immediately started praising God. We praised God like the tumor was gone and the doctor had given me a clean bill of health. There was no waiting for the battle to be over to proclaim the victory. We praised him in advance.

God being the great God that He is confirmed His word just for me. My son notified a friend of mine in California about the diagnosis. When I finally talked to her, she said she was at work when my son called; the news shook her up so badly she had to step away from her desk. She went outside, got in her car, and cried. After pulling herself together, she was about to pray for me, and that's when the spirit of the Lord told her not to pray but to praise.

When she told me that, I could hardly believe it! It was confirmation for me that God really wanted me to stop praying and start praising. There she was in California receiving the same word I had received and shared in Arizona. She didn't know God had instructed me to share that with the congregation. It was absolutely amazing to me how God did that. All of this transpired after being told the tumor was wrapped around the orbit.

MRI #4: Another three months passed, and it was time for MRI number four. As usual, the MRI was done one week before seeing the doctor. At this appointment, the doctor walked into the room, and he had a larger than usual smile on his face. He looked at me, never stopped smiling, and said, "Evelyn, I've got some good news for you. The tumor is dead! It is inactive. The shell is still there, but everything that was living inside the shell is dead. It might take a few months or up to a year, but the shell will dissolve."

All I could do at that moment was thank God. The staff in the doctor's office got so excited and congratulated me. I thanked them, but my focus was on giving God the glory for what He did for me. It was finally my day to receive my miracle! This was the day that had been prayed, praised, and believed for! My heart was filled with so much gratitude to my heavenly Father. I could not stop praising him.

Walking out of the office on the way to my car, tears of joy streamed down my cheeks. I got in and just sat there crying and praising God. The song playing in the car was so appropriate for that moment. It kept repeating how amazing God is. I cried and worshiped all the way home.

When I looked back over the process, I realized that just three months before I was healed the devil tried to make things look worse with the report that the tumor was wrapped around my orbit.

It was right in the midst of a bad situation looking worse when the Lord said, "Stop praying and start praising." Then miraculously three months later, that same tumor that was wrapped around the orbit was dead. What a mighty God we serve! There is none like Him in all the earth! I'm a living witness that if you believe in God, all things are possible.

I couldn't wait to share the incredible news with family and friends and those who had prayed and praised for me. I was flying to Arkansas for my mother's eighty-first birthday celebration in a couple of days and thought that would be a great time to share the good news with family members. Who knew that would be the last time I would see my mom alive? That was in the month of February. My husband passed away just three months later. My heart was filled with thankfulness over the fact that they both witnessed the miracle God performed in my life.

My mother was no stranger to miracles. She experienced a few of her own. The biggest one was when doctors sent her home to die with stage four pressure wounds. They said the infection was in her bones, and the wounds would never heal. Because she was a woman of unwavering faith, not only did the wounds heal, but she lived another seven years after being sent home to die. What an incredibly awesome God!

God Working in Mysterious Ways

One Saturday night, the Lord impressed upon me to visit a church on Sunday that I had never attended before. I couldn't imagine why the pull on my spirit was so strong. There was no shaking it. I didn't know anyone there but went anyway. It was uncomfortable walking into a place where I didn't know anyone and had no idea why God sent me there. When the pastor got up, he talked about how he had a message prepared, but God woke him up in the middle of the night and changed it. He didn't understand why, but he obeyed.

When he gave the title of his message, I didn't fully understand, but it gave me a clue as to why God sent me there. He said, "The title of my message is How to Get Your Healing." During the message, he stopped to give a word of knowledge. He said, "Someone has a tumor and is getting ready to have an MRI. The MRI is going to show that the tumor is gone. It is going to be dissolved! I don't care what the doctor says. God told me to tell you that He is going to dissolve that tumor." The minute he said that, I knew my steps had been ordered by the Lord. I knew he was talking about me, and that God had him change his message just for me. By obeying God and attending that service, I was encouraged, my faith was increased, and everything that the Spirit of the Lord had already spoken to me concerning my healing was confirmed. That experience taught me that sometimes to get what God has for you requires stepping out of your comfort zone. Sometimes we get so use to doing the same thing the same way that we will not obey when God is leading us in a different direction.

I didn't stick around after the service but called the church the following Wednesday to ask about how to get the message from Sunday. The person on the line told me I could come by the church before Bible study was over to get a copy. I started giving my testimony to the person on the other end of the line, explaining how blessed the service was and how the word of knowledge was for me. I asked him to share that with the pastor for me. He asked for my name. I told him, and he said, "Evelyn, you're talking to the pastor." We both laughed about it. He told me that he never answers the phone on Wednesday night because he was usually in the sanctuary preparing to teach by the time I called. It was no coincidence that I visited that church and that the pastor was the one to answer the phone when I called. He asked if he could pray for me. I said yes, and he did. He told me to come to the church, and he would make sure I got a copy of the message.

I went to the church and stayed until Bible study was over. The pastor introduced himself to me and gave me the message. He asked me to promise him that when God healed me I would come back and share my testimony. When God healed me, he invited me to share at his 20th Pastoral Anniversary Celebration, and I accepted. The entire chain of events was very unusual, but sometimes God works in unusual ways. Are we willing to follow instruction when the instructions don't make sense, or when they take us out of our normal routine, or out of our comfort zone? Sometimes it is a test of obedience. Without obedience, who knows if that door would have opened for me to share that God is a healer and encourage others to believe. We never know what avenue God will use to bless us. It might not be the way we expect.

Another unusual thing happened at a church service where the speaker was someone I did not know and had never heard of. When he finished preaching, he started walking through the audience and ministering to different individuals. He walked over, pointed his hand at me, and said, "God said tell them they can stop planning your funeral because you are going to live and not die. About eight months ago, something hit your body, but God said He is going to give you a brand new body, and He is going to give you your glory (hair) back, and it's going to be longer and prettier than ever." At that particular time, it had indeed been eight months since I had received the diagnosis. Once again God was encouraging me and confirming his word through a total stranger. All I could do was give God praise for being so mindful of me.

I Know What it Looks Like

BUT I CHOOSE TO BELIEVE GOD

First and foremost, this is a testament to the lifesaving and life-changing power of God. All glory and all praise belongs to Him. There is absolutely no one else that could have healed the inoperable tumor that was on my brain. I will never stop telling my story and never stop praising God.

The readers should know that God specializes in things that seem impossible, and He can do what no other power can do. A prime example of choosing to believe God rather than what a situation looks like is found in Romans 4:19-21: "And being not weak in faith, he considered not his own body now dead, when he was about a hundred years old, and neither yet the deadness of Sarah's womb. He staggered not at the promise of God through unbelief; but was strong in faith, giving glory to God; And being fully persuaded that, what he had promised, he was able also to perform."

Through those verses, God grew my faith and gave me a message and a mantra that I still hold on to. "I know what it looks like, but I choose to believe God." That is my message and my mantra.

The first thing that caught my attention was that Abraham did not consider circumstances. He was not worried about the fact that Sarah's womb had never birthed anything or that she was past childbearing age. Nor did he consider his age and that his body was no longer young and virile. Looking at this in a natural way between the two of them, everything needed to produce the promise (a child) was unable to function like it needed to in order to produce life. Nothing about their current state looked conducive to the promise, and yet the Bible says, "He considered not." He knew what it looked like, but he chose to believe God. He believed God more than circumstances.

It was his faith that enabled him to see beyond what he and Sarah were working with and believe God anyhow.

When God makes a promise, there is no need to consider circumstances because they are not a factor when it comes to God bringing a promise to pass. He can change circumstances in an instant. It is not our job to figure out how or when it will happen. The promises of God are not like store coupons. His promises don't have an expiration date. We only need to believe that if God said it, then it's going to happen! According to Numbers 23:19, "God is not a man, that he should lie, neither the son of man, that he should repent: hath he said, and shall he not do it? Or hath he spoken, and shall he not make it good?" Knowing this, trusting God should not be an issue.

It goes on to talk about how Abraham, "staggered not at the promise of God through unbelief; but was strong in faith, giving glory to God." Staggering is a form of instability. You cannot vacillate between faith and doubt and expect God to move. James 1:8 declares, "A double minded man is unstable in all his ways.

Abraham's faith was solid. He stood firm on what he believed. It even says he was giving glory to God. If you notice, he was giving glory while he was standing strong in faith. He had not received the promise at that time, but he was already giving God glory. You can't wait for it to happen before you decide to give God glory. Give Him glory in advance. Let Him know you trust Him. Let Him know His word is good with you.

Abraham was totally convinced. "And being fully persuaded that, what he had promised, he was able also to perform." A conviction that you cannot be dissuaded from. After coming to grips and getting myself together, I became totally convinced that God would heal me. There was nothing anyone could say or do to change that or dissuade me from my belief. Rest in the fact that God is able to do just what He said He would do. He's able to perform what He promised.

As I concluded looking at this passage, the magnitude of this miracle hit me. Only God can take two dead things, bring them together, and produce a life! A child, the promised seed, came from a womb that had never produced anything. Even in the season when reproduction would have been a normal part of life, Sarah did not conceive. At an age when Abraham was young and virile, it didn't happen. Can you see the magnitude of the miracle? What God did was incredible.

Even when they tried to work their own plan with bringing Ishmael (Genesis 16:11-12) into the picture, God still had a plan for them, and it was going to happen exactly the way He planned for it to happen. His plan didn't change for them even when they tried to change it. It is mandatory to trust God enough to let him be God and demonstrate His greatness in you and through you. He gave Abraham and Sarah what He had promised years before. This story is a great example of what faith in God can do.

My desire is to see someone's faith grow to the point

where they can believe that with God all things are possible and receive whatever it is they need. It doesn't matter what the circumstances look like, and it doesn't matter if the odds are stacked against you. Don't consider any of that. Stay focused on the promise keeper; stay focused on the healer knowing that there is nothing too hard for God.

Sometimes we call our case hard, but what we are calling hard is nothing for God. In 2 Kings Chapter 3, there is a story where the Lord performs a miracle of filling a dry valley with water without making it rain. After the miracle is performed, the Bible says, "And this is but a light thing in the sight of the Lord (2 Kings 3:28)." Our hard is God's easy. You might need to change what you are calling your issue.

I never thought to call a tumor on my brain a light thing, but if filling a dry valley with water and no rain is called a light or an easy thing, maybe I need to change what I'm saying and how I am seeing things.

Through this experience, my faith for healing reached a level that I never would have believed possible. That is the level of faith I want operating in every area of my life. Not just when it comes to healing but for everything. God has given me the ability to boldly stand in complete confidence when it comes to healing. It is something that God put inside of me, and it works in my life as well as the lives of others.

To be a recipient of a miraculous healing by the power of God is an incredibly beautiful thing. I am not ashamed to tell my story. It is my belief that God will use this testimony to build faith and to touch and change lives. I trust Him so much that I give Him glory in advance for everything He is going to do and for every life He is going to touch and change.

It all starts and ends with faith in God; from receiving salvation to receiving healing, deliverance, and miracles; Faith is a requirement. "But without faith it is impossible to please Him, for he who comes to God must believe that He is, and that He is a rewarder of those who diligently seek Him" (Hebrews 11:6, NKJV).

It does not matter what your challenge is or how long it has existed with faith in God all things are possible.